A Guide to Teach You How to Live for God

First Edition

Published and Edited by My Out Loud, LLC-Latoya Out Loud!®

Design and Illustration by Zoe Ranucci, www.GoodDharma.com

Printed by KDP Kids

ISBN: 978-0-692-17968-0

C.R.A.V.E. to be B.O.L.D.

C.R.A.V.E. to be B.O.L.D.

C – Character

R – Respect

A – Attitude

V – Value

E – Education

Say it Out Loud!

I will have Godly character
I will respect God
I will have a Godly attitude
I will value God
I will educate myself and study God's word

Crave what's right, good and true

B – Be it

O – Own it

L – Live it

D – Do it

Say it Out Loud!

I will be who God has called me to be
I will own my story and my victory
I will live according to God's standards
I will do what God has called me to do

Boldly apply God's word to your life

Character

The word character can be defined as the behavior that distinguishes a person or group. This includes moral strength, integrity, reputation and other attributes. Your character is being advertised to the world daily. In the same way companies create commercials to advertise their products, God wants to use your life to advertise His word. He used His Son Jesus as an example to advertise how you should live.

Obedience. Jesus obeyed God. Do your best to obey God's every word. John 6:38 says *Jesus came down from heaven not to do his own will but to do the will of his Father.* You are free to make your own decisions but if you love God, you will do what He says. ***Here are some of the benefits of obedience and the consequences of disobedience:***

Benefits of obedience

- Confidence
- Peace
- Happiness
- Access
- Fulfilled promises
- Blessings
- Favor
- Freedom
- Wisdom
- Answered prayers
- Joy
- Safety
- Victory

Consequences of disobedience

- Worry
- Stress
- Confusion
- Anxiety
- Discord
- Punishment

According to the Bible, if you obey God and do what's right in His eyes, things will go well for you.

Service. Jesus was a servant. Matthew 20:28 says *Jesus did not come to be served, but to serve, and to give his life as a ransom for many.* He didn't allow anything to stand in the way of serving God's purpose. He died on the cross so that you would not die in sin, which is the greatest service of all. Like Jesus, you are here to serve God's purpose. He wants you to serve with love, joy, patience, peace, kindness, gentleness, self-control, goodness and faithfulness. These are called the fruit of the Spirit, which are a representation of God's love for you.

Love is included in the fruit of the Spirit found in Galatians 5:22-23. Let's take a look at what God says about love.

1 Corinthians 13:4-7 NIV teaches us the right way to love.
Fill in the Blank.

Love is __patient__, love is __kind__. It does not __envy__, it does not __boast__, it is not __proud__. It does not ____________ others, it is not ____________, it is not easily ____________, it keeps no ____________ of ____________. Love does not ____________ in ____________ but rejoices with the ____________. It always protects, always ____________, always ____________, always ____________.

We have been called to serve each other in love and to love our neighbor as we love ourselves.
Galatians 5:13-14

Respect

Putting God first means that you will respect what's important to Him. For instance, He says to forgive others in the same way that He forgives you. If you're not willing to practice forgiveness, then you're not respecting God.

You must choose to set aside your own desires and live respectably. Making decisions that will strengthen your mind, body and soul will help you build a deeper connection with God.

Mind: Pray, read and study the Bible, practice what you learn and ask questions

Body: Eat well, exercise and create healthy habits

Soul: ALL OF THE ABOVE

God also wants you to respect those He has placed in authority. In the Bible, He has instructed you to honor your father and mother as well as submit to governing authorities. It doesn't say honor them if they treat you right; it simply says honor and submit. Ultimately, in spite of how you feel about those in authority, respect God by respecting them. People in authority can include teachers, coaches, police, judges, pastors, the President and more.

RESPECT GOD

R – Reverence – Honor and obey Him

E – Engage – Share His word

S – Study – Learn about Him

P – Pray – Communicate with Him

E – Examine – Observe His ways

C – Create – Use the gifts and talents He has given you

T – Trust – Rely on Him

Attitude

God desires for you to have an attitude of faith. Faith is not based on what you can prove, but on your confidence in God. Some people have to see to believe, but the faithful believe without seeing. For instance, the Bible says that God raised Jesus from the dead. A faithful person believes these events are true even without witnessing the act.

Having faith in God's word is power to change your mind and emotions.

Tired? Faith says God will be your strength.
(The Lord is my strength and my shield. Psalm 28:7)

Sad? Faith says God will fill you with joy.
(May the God of hope fill you with all joy
and peace as you trust in him. Romans 15:13)

Uncertain? Faith says that God will give you direction.
(I will instruct you and teach you in the way you should go. I will counsel you with my loving eye upon you. Psalm 32:8)

Hebrews 11:1 says *faith is the substance of things hoped for and the evidence of things not seen.* Just because you can't touch, feel, hear, see, taste or smell it, it doesn't mean it's not real. 2 Corinthians 5:7 says *walk by faith and not by sight.* For example, if you're praying for something that seems impossible, don't look at the circumstances, just believe that what you've been praying for will come to pass. God's word is the only evidence you need.

Circumstance	Hope	Evidence
You feel sad	You desire joy	*Do not grieve for the joy of the Lord is your strength.* Nehemiah 8:10
You feel hopeless	You desire confidence	*Come to me, all you who are weary and burdened, and I will give you rest.* Matthew 11:28
You feel afraid	You desire peace	*Do not fear for I am with you; do not be dismayed, for I am your God. I will strengthen you and help you; I will uphold you with my righteous right hand.* Isaiah 41:10
You feel discouraged	You desire courage	*Be strong and courageous. Do not be afraid; do not be discouraged, for the Lord your God will be with you wherever you go.* Joshua 1:9

Value

God values His relationship with you. When someone accepts Jesus as their Lord and Savior, he or she become a member of God's family. Naturally, a child learns to value the standards set by his or her parents. In the same way, when entering God's family, you will learn to value His standards. If you humbly submit to God and value Him, you will obtain His favor. James 4:6 says *God opposes the proud and gives grace to the humble.*

Humble:

1. Not being proud or haughty; not being arrogant or assertive
2. Reflecting, expressing, or being offered in a spirit of submission
3. Ranking low in hierarchy or scale

Jesus humbly submitted to God and valued His thoughts. You must have the same humility.

REFUSE TO

Think

Act

Move

Go

or

Be

WITHOUT GOD!

Proud:

1. Being arrogant or assertive
2. Being conceited or having an excessive self-esteem
3. Conceited or an excessive appreciation of one's own worth

There's nothing wrong with having confidence, but confidence without God's guidance can turn into arrogance and conceit. Those who believe in themselves more than God will fail because nothing will last without Him.

Education

2 Timothy 3:16 says *all scripture is God-breathed and is useful for teaching, rebuking, correcting and training in righteousness.* The fact that scripture is God-breathed means that every word is alive! Hebrews 4:12 says *the word of God is alive and active.* His words are not just to be admired on paper, but to be put into action and used daily. This is why you must pray, study and educate yourself in order to know what He desires. Here are 4 steps to follow when studying:

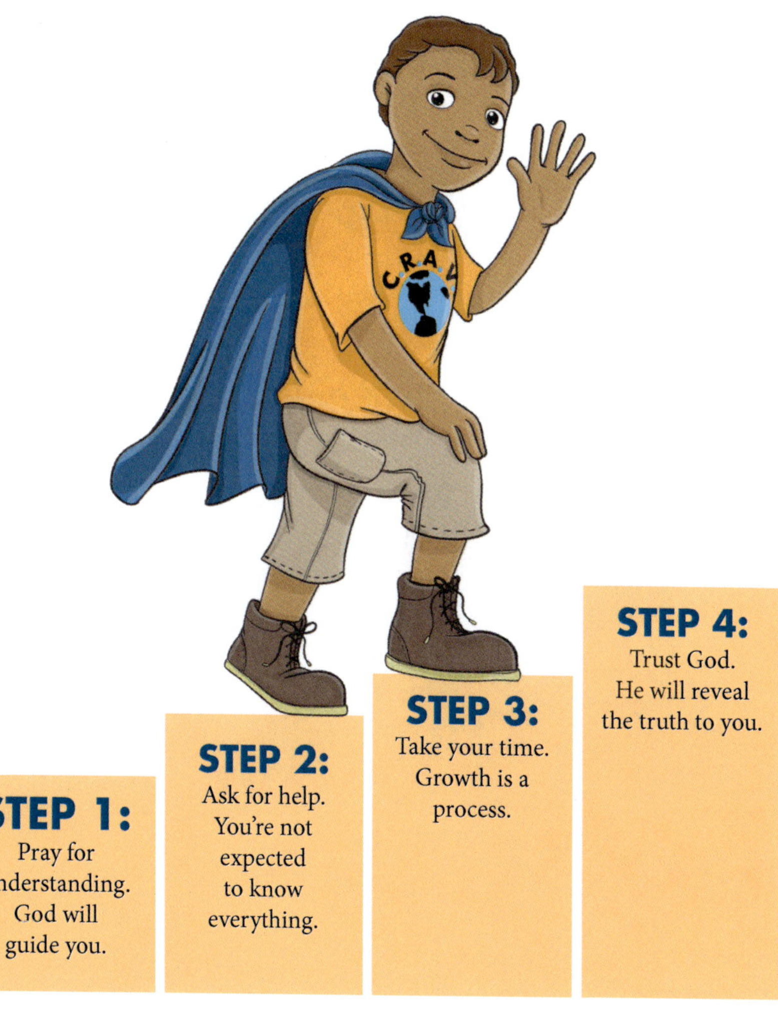

B.O.L.D.

Be it. Own it. Live it. Do it.

Be it.
Own it.
Live it.
Do it.

Be it.

You've learned to crave God's *Character*, to *Respect* Him, to have His *Attitude*, to *Value* a relationship with Him and to crave *Education*. Now let's talk about how to be who God has called you to be in this world.

The 3C's

Be **Confident**. God will act on your behalf.

Be **Certain**. His word is true.

Be **Courageous**. He is with you.

In the Bible, God trusted Joshua to lead the Israelites. Although he hadn't led them before, he put his confidence in God and obeyed Him.

Here's what God said to Joshua:

No one will be able to stand against you all the days of your life. As I was with Moses, so I will be with you; I will never leave nor forsake you. Be strong and courageous, because you will lead these people to inherit the land I swore to their ancestors to give them. Joshua 1:5-9.

Joshua was placed in an unfamiliar situation and had to rely on God for direction. It could be assumed that he may have experienced doubt and fear but most importantly, he didn't allow his emotions to stop him from trusting God.

God is with you just as He was with Joshua, but be aware that Satan wants to strip you of your confidence. He does this by arousing your emotions and feeding you untruthful words and ideas that will convince you to give up. He wants you to think that you will never make it, that God has forgotten you, that you're alone, that no one believes in you, and that life is better without you. This is his way of attempting to distract you from being who God has called you to be in life.

Here's how to stay focused:

Be Vigilant

Be keenly watchful to detect danger,
stay awake and be on constant alert

In Mark 14:38, Jesus warns his disciples to watch and to pray so that they won't fall into temptation. Temptation is the desire to do something wrong or unwise. Satan wants you to desire what pleases your flesh instead of what pleases God. Here are some things the flesh will desire over God:

Money
Fame
Drugs

Power
Self-pleasure
Food

Honestly, these can be used for good or bad. It's left up to you to determine how you will use them. For example, you need food to live, but overindulging will lead to health issues. Galatians 5:17 says *the flesh desires what is contrary to the Spirit, and the Spirit what is contrary to the flesh.*

Be Excellent

Possessing outstanding quality or superior merit; Being remarkably good

Excellence starts in the mind and manifests into reality. Satan wants you to worry, but God wants you to have His thoughts. Philippians 4:8 says *whatever is true, whatever is noble, whatever is right, whatever is pure, whatever is lovely, whatever is admirable-if anything is excellent or praiseworthy-think about such things.* If you think on the things mentioned in Philippians, there's no room for worry.

What have you thought about lately? Are your thoughts mostly positive or negative? Learn God's word so that you can replace the negative thoughts with His truth. You have the power to change the way you think.

Here's an example:

Thought: I'm ugly

Truth: According to Psalm 139:14, you are fearfully and wonderfully made in God's image.

Be Silent

The absence of any sound or noise; stillness.

Go to a quiet place where you can hear from God. Jeremiah 29:11 says *God has plans to prosper you and not to harm you, plans to give you hope and a future.* Have you ever had to put a toy together? The picture on the box revealed what it should look like but in order for it to look like what was on the box, you had to follow the directions. If you want to live the life God has planned for you, you have to follow His directions. The trees, the flowers, the sun and the moon are all evidence that proves He's the best planner and creator of all time. His plan for your life is greater than what you can imagine. Ask Him to remove the unnecessary noise blocking you from hearing Him clearly.

Unnecessary noise can come from people, places, things or anything that take you away from giving God your undivided attention. Be responsible and limit the amount of time you spend on distracting activities.

Find	→	a quiet place
Listen	→	to God's direction
Receive	→	His instruction and plan

Own it.

No matter what you've experienced, you need to *face it and embrace it.* The ups and downs, the good and bad, the defeats and the victories all play a part in your story. You need to own every tear cried, every mistake made and every lesson learned. When you own it, you take away Satan's power to use it against you.

For example, being hurt as a child may lead to trust issues. Satan can use distrust as a weapon of isolation. This is why facing and embracing past experiences is important. If you can identify what hurt you, you can make the decision to release it. If you don't own it, it will own you. ***Follow the example below and fill in each scenario.***

Own Your Story	Own Your Victory
Ex: I'm disappointed… because my grades are not good.	**Ex: But...I'm studying harder to make better grades.**
I cry when I think about…	But…
This person hurt me when…	But…
I gave up because…	But…

Live it.

To live a righteous and prosperous life, you must let go of unhealthy relationships, environments and habits. Jesus told the disciples to deny themselves and to follow Him. Just like the disciples, you're expected to deny yourself of the things that prevent you from following God wholeheartedly.

Relationships: Engage with those who support your spiritual growth and respect your decision to live for God.

Environments: Stay away from people, places and environments that cause you to be distracted.

Habits: Be aware of old patterns that interrupt your development.

Relationships	Environments	Habits
Who are the people that support your spiritual growth?	Where do you feel safe?	What old patterns are you aware of?

Do it.

Congratulations!

You made it. You are now equipped with the knowledge that will help you grow in your relationship with God. At this point, you have the opportunity to decide how to put all you've learned into action. James 1:22 says *don't just listen to the word; do what it says.* Listed on the next page are a few things God has called you to do. Write down how you will fulfill each one.

How will you ***serve*** God?

How will you ***give*** to your community?

How will you ***encourage*** others?

How will you ***pray*** for your family and friends?

How will you ***create*** a God-centered life?

How will you ***love*** your enemies?

How will you ***engage*** others in God's word?

How will you ***listen*** to those in authority?

Here are other things you can do to serve God's purpose:

- Volunteer at a shelter
- Go on a mission trip
- Plan a community project
- Make a donation
- Start a prayer group

Remember, you are not on the earth by chance.

God sent you to C.R.A.V.E. to be B.O.L.D.

"Go into all the world and preach the gospel to all creation."

Mark 16:15

The Crave Creed

The creed will remind you to think and to interact positively. You should learn, memorize and repeat the creed each day.

Character

My character plays a major role
in how I am perceived by society.

Respect

I will have respect for myself and others.
If I give respect, I will get respect.

Attitude

My attitude can take me a long way.
I will stay positive and reach my goals.
A negative attitude can only lead to failure.

Value

I value my own self-worth and
know the importance of family values.
If I don't stand for something,
I will fall for anything.

Education

My mental and moral growth is very important.
Knowledge is the key to success,
and I am the key to the future.

GOD → The Father

Creator • Ruler • Wise
Powerful • Perfect • All-knowing

When you accept Jesus as Lord, you accept God as your Father.

JESUS → The Son

Christ • Messiah • Anointed One
Savior • Light of the world • Head of the church

Jesus represents God's character, image and being.

HOLY SPIRIT → The Helper

Spirit of God • Spirit of Truth • Counselor
Advocate • Guide • Teacher

The Holy Spirit lives in you
and helps you make decisions that please God.

YOU → The Vessel

Chosen • Beloved • Redeemed
Body of Christ • Child of God • Kingdom Citizen

God created you to do good works in the earth
that bring Him glory.

DECLARE

If you declare with your mouth, "Jesus is Lord," and believe in your heart that God raised him from the dead, you will be saved. For it is with your heart that you believe and are justified, and it is with your mouth that you profess your faith and are saved. As scripture says, "Anyone who believes in him will never be put to shame."

Romans 10:9-11

BELIEVE

An important element to having a relationship with God is believing in His Son Jesus Christ. This means, you need to believe every word the Bible says about Him.

Here are a few things the Bible says about Jesus:

- He was in the beginning with God (John 1:1-2).
- All things were made through Him (John 1:3).
- He's the word that became flesh (John 1:14).
- He takes away the sin of the world (John 1:29).
- He is one with God (John 10:30).
- He is the only way to the Father (John 14:6).
- He died on the cross for our sins (John 19:30).
- He rose from the dead (John 20:11-18).

RECEIVE

The gift of grace was given to you because of what Jesus did for you.

1. He died on the cross.
2. God raised Him from the dead.
3. Eternal life has been given through Him.

Choose to *declare* Jesus as Lord and Savior,
believe in your heart and *receive* the gift of eternal life.

Now, take a moment to write it down.

When you are done, say it Out Loud!

I declare...

___

___

I believe...

___

___

I receive...

___

___

FOR
GOD
DID
NOT

SEND HIS SON INTO THE
WORLD TO CONDEMN
THE WORLD, BUT TO

SAVE
THE
WORLD
THROUGH
HIM

JOHN 3:17

* MOSES HID HIS FACE IN THE CLEFT OF THE ROCK.

* THE ROCK = JESUS = THE WORD BECAME FLESH = BIBLE

* READING THE WORD = HIDING OUR FACE IN THE CLEFT OF THE ROCK

Made in the USA
Columbia, SC
03 April 2019